Arch Hades

FOOL'S GOLD

Poetry and Postcards

AUSTIN MACAULEY PUBLISHERS™

LONDON • CAMBRIDGE • NEW YORK • SHARJAH

A CIP catalogue record for this title is available from the British Library.

ISBN 9781528987950 (Paperback)
ISBN 9781528987967 (ePub e-book)

www.austinmacauley.com

First Published (2020)
Austin Macauley Publishers Ltd
25 Canada Square
Canary Wharf
London
E14 5LQ

All cruelty springs from weakness

- Seneca

Poetry & Postcards
Volume 2

Fool's Gold

Index

Part 1: Poetry

Part 2: Postcards

Itsukushima, Japan

Kyushu, Japan

Shimane, Japan

Osaka, Japan

Sado, Japan

Bergen, Norway

County Clare, Ireland

Chambretaud, France

Chicago, USA

Montana, USA

Bermuda

Seville, Spain

Barcelona, Spain

Bedfordshire, UK

Miami, USA

Rome, Italy

Burano, Italy

Venice, Italy

Part 1
Poetry

Anticipation

My beautiful maybe, my great perhaps
The heat of my imagination
Captures us, as we elapse
In restrained, delicate elation

Walls echo in your absence
Another brief sojourn
I'll wreck myself against infinity
In re-doubled lust, I slowly burn

Night after night my mind orbits
Around you, my sun, my star
Anticipation, blazing like a comet
Confined to watch you from afar

My new beginning,
The one that hasn't come
I ache over agonising details
Over you, my song unsung

My future, I believe impending
I am a thief of pleasure,
Fantasies, recklessly spending
Our delights, we have not measured

Our moonlit elopements,
The ones that haven't passed
My conspiracy of silence
I've committed to steadfast

My flame imperishable
You've rekindled all that's earnest
And even though you burn me so
My hope in us will spring eternal

Lucky charm

I look at you
I want more time
To spend it all
Within your arms
I need to be
The one you need
To make you smile
Your lucky charm

Eyes like clear honey

Eyes like clear honey, when that sunlight hits
They pierce my soul, my heart to you, submits
Drunk on your beauty, much past my limits
I gladly stay for days in our minutes

It's meaningless, I've only lived for you
My open heart for you to take and do,
Whatever begs your will, love or subdue
Till you decide, in ache, I wait for you

I'll savour every detail of sublime
Committing to my memory, your prime
Forever young, with me you'll stay divine
Love's paragon, within my mind's confines

Gravity

Your gravity, it's pulling me
Further from my sanity
To a blissful agony

Willingly, I will descend
We both know, without pretend
It's too late for this to end

I start to hear music whenever you're around

Gambler

I am a gambler, always live in hope
I think I'll chance my heart once more
Your luck, my token, will defy the house
And soon, we'll share our winning score

If ardor overflows your cup
It is senseless being prudent
To let love out, and let love in
Highest accolade of humans

And even if I lose it all,
I'll carry on with no regrets
No such a thing as wasted love,
I am a gambler, don't forget

Sheer lightness of your being
While others burn, you shine

Wanting

My love for you will never tire,
Nor will it fade, decrease, expire
My whole life, I'll devote to you
If only you'll allow me to
I cannot make you want me more
Despite how much that I'll adore

Delicate

My heavy heart strains in my chest
And speeds up when I'm pondering
Of you, of us, this power's enough
To be my own undoing

How will it end? Will it begin?
High on my anticipation
It keeps me burning up within
My faith in quiet restoration

Will I chase these dreams so long
That they'll turn into my nightmares?
Or will you turn to me and say
The words that echo in my prayers?

John Green

You said if people were like rain
You'd be a drizzle and I, a hurricane
And in that storm, we both got caught
No looking back, no second thoughts

More than scarlet

You told me you loved me, you silently cried
Said this is real for you, for the first time
You promised on you, I could always rely
You kissed me and placed, your hand in mine

I'll give you my best, and all I can be
To my heart's kingdom, I'll grant you the key
I promise you'll never be lonely like me
I hope that you soar, that love sets you free

My second adolescence, you make me feel alive
So young and indestructible, infinite, sublime

Three months later

Your heart, the wave-beat of a troubled sea
The first whisper of our tragedy

Symmetry

How can we love so differently?
To you it seems a tedious chore
To me it comes so naturally
I will at liberty do more

I want to take you everywhere
To all the corners of my mind
I give myself so willingly
Just want to fill your life with light

Waiting up for your late nights
You present your pale excuses
I turn to you, you turn away
Your love for me nightly reduces

When I need most your sweet relief
It's the last thing you want to give
Feels like I'm always chasing you
Say you love me, but is it true?

It's always me who's reaching out
Lifting you up, expelling doubt
How I love you, you don't love me
This love is far from symmetry

You call it love, but I don't recognise it

Fair-weather love

You only love me in the light
You only love that side of me
When everything's a rosy haze
You only want it easily

Not everything's so perfect
What about when it gets hard?
My flaws and imperfections
You run away when it gets dark

This love's too hard for you it seems
Telling me to 'hold my tongue'
When I dare to disagree, you sneer
'Why can't you just be fun?'

Judge me when you're perfect
Preaching your moral absolutes
Don't talk down at me like that
Ignoring problems when it suits

How dare I have my own opinions?
How dare I voice my inner thoughts?
Your intolerant, fair-weather love
Will eat away at us and rot

Left unsaid

Some things you can't un-do
Some words you can't un-say
Does your anger reveal truths?
Thoughts you hid away?

When you've delivered all your blows
When your heat cools to regret
I may forgive you, but you know
Some things I can't forget

It's the ones that we let in, that can destroy us from within

Cardinal sin

Parched soil of our mutual desire
Carnal delights lead to cardinal sins
Awaiting promises expire
Think what you'll end if this begins

Your wounded innocence you preach
With subdued violence, you continue
Unfaithful absence I impeach
Your lethal lust, the death of us

The jealous type

You know I'm not the jealous type
I don't care who looks at you
So long as I have your attention
You'll have all of mine too

But you flirt with other women
Trying so hard to impress
It doesn't make me jealous
It just makes me like you less

Vain

You gave away the things I loved
And one of them was you
To all of those who wanted some
Regardless if it's due

Your crowded heart and fickle mind
Charmed by validation
Overlooking your commitment
Addicted to attention

You say you're mine, but every time
My nerves quietly fray
As you embrace the whole world while
It's me you hide away

Play me

You weaponised my happiness
Used it for your 'art'
Agony to hear you speak my words
My words, they all came from my heart

You sing them like they're meaningless
You don't feel their real pain
Just get on stage and afterwards
You play me once again

Spoonful

You give me enough to last one more day
A spoonful of love postpones our decay
Beg me to never, from you walk away
And promise enough, to make sure I stay

Faithless

A love so sweet that soured all too quickly
You rushed to have me, then you rushed to leave
Our love's myth, kept alive by the faithful
Fades as quickly if you cease to believe

Innocence lost and paradise wilting
Our creed is doomed with just one devotee
Our church's haunted to me if you jilt it
Are you breaking me to simply break free?

Resigned

'We' didn't end when I left
'We' ended when you quit trying
The moment you stopped listening
We switched to borrowed time

Real love won't make you feel unwanted

Overpromise

No one 'set you up to fail'
No one made you overpromise
Don't take this out on me
With yourself you're not being honest

You say things you do not mean
Then blame my 'expectations'
Stop making promises and fix
Your poor communication

True colours

You say you love me less
Whenever I 'talk back'
I'm searching in your eyes
Now how should I react?

Threaten and control me
When I dare not agree
You can't just take it back
You're taking liberties

I see your true colours,
Shining through so bright
Unmasked once again,
What a hideous sight

Once they can't control you, they'll try to control
how others see you

Fiction

You're the source of your fiction, can't handle the truth
Preaching lies, your addiction, your guilt they will soothe

You re-write events, save your holy depiction
But you give to yourself, the biggest restriction

You annul the sins, that could cause you pain
But rob yourself of some learning, some gain

You repeat your lies till they become true
Fool everyone, but the main fool is you

Dorian Gray

Does wounding me make you feel better?
Painting me in false red letters?
Dim my lights, so you shine brighter?
Burden me, so you feel lighter?
Take my hand, take me for granted
Just be careful what you've started
I've seen what you are, the true you
The monster you hide, in plain view
Afraid of your own refection
You attempt every deflection
You play games, you try to deceive
Your own dangerous lies you believe
While all your sins, I have absorbed
You are convinced you are absolved
But a time will come, and you'll have to face,
Your transgressions, you will have to embrace
The portrait of you, projected on me
The day you'll realise with great clarity
It'll be the day of your grand dismay
And you will perish, my Dorian Gray

I wanted to believe in you so much
I started lying to myself

Fool's gold

You must think yourself enchanting
The way you cast your spells
Incantations you're supplanting
Pure embellishment and bells

All your demi-truths and white lies
I see you smile and hide your ghosts
Convinced it's such a clever guise
You're in the emperor's new clothes

You must think yourself so clever
So important, so demure
But in your trivial endeavours
I'm afraid there's no allure

All this pyrite, you're concealing
Soon they'll know, as I foretold
Time will strip your mask, revealing
You are nothing but fool's gold

Crazy

Don't call me crazy, when you're the reason why
It's getting so difficult for me to even try
To reason with your 'logic', when none of it makes sense
You don't ever listen, you don't even pretend

I can't navigate your waters, when you keep changing maps
I'm tired and defenceless, and yet you still attack
You love me inconsistently, you don't know what you need
So difficult to follow, someone who cannot lead

The issue when we fight
I want to solve the problem
and you just want to be right

Where is your mind?

Go chain-smoke to the Pixies, I don't care anymore
No need for your lectures, I've heard them before

You shut out the world, it's done you no wrong
You've never had problems, you've always belonged

You just love attention, and pray on those willing
To tell them your story, pretend that it's thrilling

You're just a brat, who has never worked hard
You have everything, but pretend your life's 'dark'

Get over yourself, you're ungrateful, entitled
Think the world owes you and everyone is your rival

Something goes wrong, you cry and you wail,
But you don't try to solve it, in case you might fail

Fragile like glass, no one can get close
Unless to caress your enormous ego

Go chain-smoke to the Pixies, pretend that you're 'cursed'
I won't indulge you, I think you're the worst

Not only will some people hurt others,
they will hate those whom they injured,
because they remind them of their flaws

Twenty-five

You think you're old at twenty-five
Without hard work, somehow, you'll thrive
The rules, to you, they don't apply
To you, we'll bow, without your try

The center of the universe
Around you, the rest must spin
Unconcerned by their opinions
Your wisdom comes from deep within

So comfortable in your convictions
But on second glance, your chains
If one questions their existence
Under pressure, you feel strained

Your brittle ears crumble in plight
Incapacitated by your ego
If you feel wronged, you turn to spite
Victimising yourself, your placebo

You backtrack on apologies
You don't mean a word you say
When you know you're 'bout to lose,
You're too quick to run away

Being on time is such a chore
You are their king; can't they just wait?
And when you finally turn up
How dare they point out that you're late!

Lose your pride or lose your love
You've been told this all before
But you've descended from above
All those 'below' you, you ignore

Paramount for you to be right
And if she leaves, it's her, not you
You're just 'so misunderstood'
Your 'genius' is a different hue

Your suffering is so unique
Oh, your wounds are full of salt!
No one's felt pain as deep as yours
And it's all somebody's fault

Folly of youth, I sympathise
We were all once that childish bore
The only problem with you is −
You're not twenty-five anymore

I tightrope I treat
Between love and hate
And I keep losing balance

Garments

You drape around me, shallow affections
Won't keep me warm, they're filled with rejections

As I beg for more garbs of attention
In your sullen eyes, strained apprehension

You take the attire, that I weaved for you
With coarse entitlement, as if it were due

For you, my love, I shape with devotion
I poured into you, warmest emotions

You take, as you scoff, complaining at me
At times love's 'too much', that it's 'too heavy'

I'd rather have that, than what you give to me
Faded, atrophied love, thin as can be

Pulling at loose strings, your love's wearing thin
But I know you'll wear me, under your skin

I'm not asking for too much, I'm asking the wrong person

And even though my heart is breaking
It is for you that it's still aching

Rain

Morning, rising without you
Slender threads of summer rain
Liquesce into my waking view,
Make tracks across my pane

Cherry blossom in the mist
Callously, each droplet hits
Like a quiet, violent tryst
Flowers, all these knocks permit

Delicate buds still rising
But with every heavy blow
Rosy petals drift a-ground
Dancing, spinning past windows

It's not within rain's nature
To be apologetic
But each collision helps me be
To you, more apathetic

I'm afraid we only have our love in common
What happens if it fades?

Red flags

Hard to switch off my heart and turn on my brain
Knew it was wrong and I'm right once again
All your red flags I ignored from the start
Was the reason it ended, why we broke apart

Would it be easier to start again?

The anglerfish

Months ago, on the day it snowed,
You confessed your dystopia
Suspended from your happiness
Succumbed to anhedonia

Your higher calling called on me
Knew at once to guarantee
To hold your heart with both my hands
Warm it up, as best as I can

Tell me, what pain made you so cruel?
I will distill it all from you
I won't let this infection spread
All your past aches, I'll help you shed

Whatever poisoned you before
I will take care and I'll adore
I'll heal your wounds, and with great care
I'll pour in so much love to spare

But I can't heal you from outside
You hear me calling, hear my plight
You drink my love, like it's your due
But banish me from seeing through

I know it's not within my right
But I can see your losing fight
If you don't ease your source of pain
Forever with you, it'll remain

Regardless how much love you drink
It'll spread there too, so please rethink
I swear I'm only trying to aid
The more I do, the more you hate

As if you savour being in pain,
Feel entitled over my strain
You seek to drain me till I'm done
Then you'll discard me and move on

To the next one, that you will trick
And you'll drain her, just like you did
To me, to all, as you see fit
All your cruelty, you'll re-emit

A thousand cuts

You give me your poison, I drink it with glee
You're not supposed to want to do that to me
Don't ask me to jump, I'll ask you how high
All you want from my love, you know I'll comply

Your life-size ghost is haunting me
Stockholm syndrome is taunting me

You keep me so close that we can't grow apart
Keep cutting me down, keep on breaking my heart
You are my madness, but I need sanity
I can't let you go, so let go of me

Leash

Only when I'm close to leaving
You say the things I want to hear
Your love, a leash, around my neck
Tightens and you draw me near

You don't love me, you're just lonely

Thorns

You picked me like a rose, enchanted
I bloomed for you, I wanted to,
To bring you happiness, undaunted

You praised sweet fragrances, fine petals
But rubbed me wrong, pricked on a thorn
Your love turned furious, unsettled

One by one, picked off my spines
I bled for you, I wanted to,
Loathing thorns once mine

With wounds unbound, began to wilt
No remorse from you, no guilt
Just harsh distain, repulsion, pain

No longer I, your rose
Just a reminder, what I once was
Blaming me for being wrong

But all roses come with thorns
Perhaps it's not a rose
You wanted, all along

Your destiny, it cheated me
Too finite, your infinity

Chains

You filled our foundations
With empty promises
I trusted every word,
A dangerous genesis

Piece by piece, we shattered
Day by day, we broke
You act like it's no matter
Like none of it's your fault

Surrounded by mere ruins,
The love that we once were
Set me free, undo your chains,
Don't want to love you anymore

You don't want me, but you don't want anyone else to have me

Unconditional

You push me far away, then wonder where I went
You do not treat me kindly, but kindness you expect?

You complain at me, after closing yourself off
I'm not fighting hard enough to break down all your walls

You treat me like your enemy, but expect to be my friend
You keep on breaking us, assuming us, I'll mend

It's not my job to raise you, and manage your emotions
You cannot be malicious and still expect devotion

You seek to keep my love with actions so equivocal
Except I'm not your mother, my love's not unconditional

Hunt to kill

I thought your lonely heart, was seeking company
Your lonely heart's a hunter, killing hungrily

What kind of love have you been taught?
What kind of horrors have you seen?
You use that word just like a leash,
A noose that tightens at your whim

I'm sorry you feel incomplete
It's not my duty to fulfil you
Find in you whatever you need
Do not use me to complete you

You are destroying half of me
So I might fit your sole half better
Without a care what you impair
In your razing, you take pleasure

The helping hand I offered you
Your mad arrogance rejected
All your anger, doubts and sadness,
You instead at me, directed

As I am, I won't appease, your exhausting hunger
Your lonely heart remains, a lonely, wandering hunter

Knelt on one knee, asked for my life

But you want a servant, not a partner, nor wife

Blame it on me

I think I'm tired. I think that's it.
You've finally worn me out
It's all too much, I can't commit
To your life of ups and downs

Every day it's something new
We can't rewind to the beginning
You douse my fire until it's blue
And all you care about is winning

Preoccupied with gaining ground
Keeping score and turning tables
At that table we sit, bound

And I just want to leave

Are you sad that you hurt me, or that you just got caught?
Are you mad at yourself, or that you have to stop?

Numb

I want to feel numb, I'm done with emotions
Can't go on swimming, drowning in oceans

Angry, yet helpless, so powerless still
Silent self-pity within me distils

I can't turn this tide, I'll wait till the dawn
And you're going to miss me, when I am gone

Fortress

When all I feel is darkness
When all my days are nights
Alone in my mind's fortress
Remind me there's a light

October

Autumn is beautiful
But everything is dying
And all I'm doing is denying
All the feelings that I'm hiding

I don't love you anymore

Amor fati

Goodbye my lover, you were never my friend
Only love as our guide, it led to dead ends

Both taxing and wanting, what we put on the line
Right from the start, our hearts beat out of time

Seasoned with sorrows, minds heavy with loss
All good intentions, destroyed in chaos

Our only redemption, without any blame
The right thing and hard thing turned out all the same

Wishes and stars

Feared fading into memory
But faced your fears and ran afar
Guess fears, like dreams, they do true
When you wish on the wrong star

And now I'm here, but without you
No Romeo to my Juliet
And just a memory you'll be,
As soon as I forget

Feeling

I had always suspected
You're in love with a feeling
But I kept on believing
That you really loved me

Time came, I, unwilling
Gave up all my dreaming
Let you go, though it's chilling
What you loved, who's to see?

Irrelevant now

Thought we had so much in common
Both straining under heavy dreams
You brag you sail with passions high
While pushing paper boats downstream

Romanticising all your plans
While chasing dreams inside your head
But nothing works, unless you do
Can't cheat yourself to get ahead

You're not a victim, you're not drowning,
You just can't be arsed to swim
The only danger is your sloth,
That you keep fueling from within

Instead of standing by my side
You tricked me into conceding
Into dimming my own light,
Feeling guilty for succeeding

You hurt me, and then complain?
You don't get it, you don't listen
Knocking haloes off my saints
Has always been your vile religion

I'm tired of carrying us both
I can't do this any longer
At least carrying your dead weight
Made me a little stronger

You've been calling, it rings out
Without a flinch of apprehension
I'll starve your ego with a drought
You don't deserve any attention

Sometimes I think I might miss you
Sometimes I doubt why I left
Then I remember the bad things
You did and how awful they felt

Go ahead, fill up my voicemail
I won't grant you one last bow
Yours fears, like my dreams, all came true
You are irrelevant now

Your name flashes, there's no fire, no heat
My heart doesn't race, tripping over, skipping beats

Say my name

Do not mistake me for your friend
Do not believe that 'we are good'
My mute departure and my grace
You seem to have misunderstood

I don't have goodwill towards you
Nor can I spare you any hate
I remember what you did
There's not a thing you can abate

I've found my peace, I'm happy now
It doesn't mean there's room for you
Do not infect me with your chaos
You've not changed since we were through

You think you shaped me in your image?
I'll never be like you, you'll see
All your poison, I've cried out,
All the hate you poured on me

I won't raise my voice or egress
From you, I'll just turn away
But don't you dare approach me,
You don't deserve to say my name

Feels good feeling nothing

Untitled

I've read our story
I think it's done
It's time to start
A different one

Gambler II

I am a gambler, always live in hope
My winning streak was cut quite short
Alas, the house, it won once more
But my beliefs, it'll never thwart

Whole, broken or breaking
My heart is always full of love
If not eros, then agape or philia
This I'll never fall short of

And even if I lose once more
I'll carry on with no regrets
No such a thing as wasted love,
I am a gambler, don't forget

Bless you, Mr Vonnegut

Standing alone in that black coat
My compassionate turquoise, my antidote
Paint my heart in a fresh hue
Help me love, as if anew

Hearts

Fragile hearts, they often break
But heal with perseverance
And their pain, they soon forget
Fragile, yet resilient

Autumn (Tannhäuser)

Wet bark aglow with gilded leaves
Chorus of rustles as they dance
A death so beautiful, I grieve
A heaving waltz, terminal trance

Shedding memories, proud celebration
Not breaking, simply breaking free
Homecoming, pre-reincarnation
We watch the world turn through these trees

Suffering, pain, all part of bliss
Enchanting beauty of the living
My heart at liberty chose this
Not bitter loss, but sweet forgiving

Accept all things I cannot change
You keep my faith, discard my scars
All of life's ends, no longer strange
My nights are low on nightmares now

Versailles (temple of love)

I saw two otters in Versailles
Among the submerged weeds they played
And dragonflies paired off and danced
And frogs called out each other's names

Cupid, shaded by the cupola
Providence forever watching
Onto the brook's wild bends and banks
Leaving all un-fallen wanting

Temple of love beaming in white
Charms all abiding to its reign
All things in sight with blooming eyes
And I believe in love again

Part 2
Postcards

Itsukushima, Japan
27 May 2018

On my way to observe the famous floating torii gate, it's noticeable that Japan is an orderly and beautiful country. Nature is deeply appreciated and every home-owning aesthete seems fastidious in their gardening. I hear it is the first day of the melon festival in Hokkaido.

Itsukushima

Kyushu, Japan
31 May 2018

Rakanji Temple was built in 645AD and has remained at its
mountain watch for centuries since. I am listening to the rain in the
valley, drinking shiitake mushroom tea in the mist. A local delicacy,
a popular item for a reason. It is potent, sweet and aromatic.

Kyushu

Shimane, Japan
2 June 2018

I am sipping a lemon tea, overlooking Adachi gardens. A large
koi carp close-by is gently nibbling away at some algae covering a
submerged rock. It's mainly white, with asymmetrical black and
orange patches. The sun is high and time feels suspended here.

Shimane

Osaka, Japan
5 June 2018

I am having a bath on the 25th floor, overlooking Osaka through a
wall of glass. It's late and a lightning storm has rolled across the city.
Flashes of amber cut through the thick, violet clouds and amplify
the skyline. I can't hear the thunder, I'm listening to the Moonlight
Sonata. It's more atmospheric this way.

Osaka

Sado, Japan

8 June 2018

I've wandered into an old sake brewery on Sado Island, but what caught my attention was a small swallows nest nestled in the roof spires above a lighting fixture. Three tiny chicks call it home.
I am content.

Sado

Bergen, Norway
1 July 2018

The composer's hut

Midsummer day, Norwegian shores
Peaceful banks brim with black sand
I stand where Grieg once stood before
Paying my tribute, hat in hand

Outside his small composer's hut
Cool waters lapping at the rocks
Like instruments, it plays them so
With muted kisses, soft echoes

Amongst the pebbles, scattered shells
Graveyard of hollow mussels
Idly sparkling in the high sun
With the gentle swell, they tussle

They tilt and sway to unseen rhythms
Of heaving tides, so faithfully
I hear what Grieg once heard before
Nature's own joyous harmony

Norway

Cliffs of Mohar, Ireland
8 July 2018

Be still, your violent winds and crashing waves of ire
Your infinite beauty, I, the finite, will admire
Grant me a moment's peace to stand still and respire
We all have but a moment, before we all expire

Shared yearning to feel, a part of something bigger
I'm not the ocean, I'm a wave, a glimmer

Into oblivion we gaze, still sailing on
Until oblivion returns our gaze, and dawns
The passage of the years, more than we want to know
Fortune gives us nothing, which we can really own

Ireland

Chambretaud, France
18 July 2018

It's overcast, but still a balmy 25C and I've just eaten the ripest apricot. I am eager to wander through the forest. I want to get tangled in your fine cobwebs, feel them brush along my skin. I want to marvel at the marbled green on your vast glassy ponds. I want to sit by your weeping willows and watch plump geese frolic in between your lily pads. We need nature, nature doesn't need us.

Chambretaud

Chicago, USA
25 July 2018

Sixteen Canada geese float by on Lake Michigan. I scan the
skyline of Chicago. Today, while attempting to recreate my own
Bueller moment while staring at Seurat's 'a Sunday afternoon'
I remembered my mother once told me that the Impressionists
rejected black, even in shadows. Once more, she is absolutely right.

Chicago

Montana, USA
2 August 2018

Granite County, population: 3,029. The air is so fresh I can
almost taste the huckleberries. The grass grows stirrup high in the
valleys and the gentle wind caresses clusters of purple daises in
the mountain meadows. Something about this big open sky really
sets the imagination off, and I am blissfully reduced to watch the
shadows of the tall pines grow longer. I'd like to stay on.

Montana

Bermuda
27 August 2018

Sitting on the beach, I watch you swim in the turquoise waters.
Above, two long-tails dance across the sky, one always pursuing the
other, the other refusing to be caught. All I do is chase you, denying
that the right one won't keep running. Suddenly, I've realised that
I'm deeply unhappy.

Bermuda

Seville, Spain
15 September 2018

When I'm with you, I dissolve, I am pure desire. And the history of
my desire for you is the story of how it blinded me.
You came back to the hotel at 4am. I hadn't slept a minute. Alone, I
heard the clock tower strike one, then two, then three. I tried to get
close to you, but you pushed me away. I fear this is our énouement.

Seville

Barcelona, Spain
16 September 2018

The next day we flew to Barcelona – the tickets you promised to book, but kept on forgetting. You scolded me every few weeks when I'd remind you, until I just quietly did it myself. Another argument ensued.

And while each argument hasn't been individually devastating enough to warrant a break up, over time, each unresolved dispute added to the lumbering sediment of sorrow, which became the real heaviness that ultimately broke us.

Barcelona

Bedfordshire, UK
October 2018

How can you sit there and tell me you love me, tell me how much
you want a future with me – but on your last night in London you'd
rather stay out till 3am getting drunk with a girl I've never heard
you mention, one I'm not allowed to meet?
You ignored me for a week prior, telling me you need 'space'. You
didn't allow me to see your show, to support you. I know it was
because you felt guilty about missing my reading, second one in a
row. You just forgot. You're not interested in what's important to
me. I know you were punishing me with your radio silence, unable
to take responsibility for yourself, you lash out instead.

Every time you broke a promise, I trusted you less. Every time you
didn't listen, I became less patient. Every time you brushed an
argument aside without resolving it with me, I became less kind. For
that I am sorry. But I don't want to be your girlfriend anymore and
I don't want to be your wife.
It's always been so simple. You want me, show me. You love me,
show me. You either want to make an effort with me or you don't.
And you don't. And I can't make you.
I don't hate you. I'm not angry. There was always a misery in you
that you clung to, regardless how much I tried to help. I realise
now it's because you believe being miserable makes you special. It
doesn't, it just makes you miserable. I hope you fix that.

Goodbye.

Bedfordshire

Miami, USA
20 December 2018

Suddenly, all my time is my own again and I don't have to spend it on you. The happiness, the peace that has flooded my life, it's a sweet release. I can breathe again.

Miami

Rome, Italy
12 March 2019

Seven hills and tall, neat pines
Ancient prayers all left behind
Wishes made on countless dimes
Eternal city of our times

Majesty in marble vanities
Treasures lost to endless atrophy
Presently, a whole new malady
Masses, most entranced in apathy

Yet, your beauty does not fade
Even if it's not surveyed
And if Rome falls to decay
Tributes we'll forever pay

Rome

Burano, Italy
17 March 2019

It is my birthday and I am spending it alone, as I intended.
As I'm eating my lunch at Riva Rosa - seafood, lightly fried with
zucchini - I observe on the adjacent window pane two pigeons in
a flirtatious dance. So curious to watch two creatures we so often
think as vile, court each other so tenderly.

Burano

Venice, Italy
17 March 2019

From Burano I boarded a water taxi to spirit me back to Venice.
On our way we passed the Isle of the Dead and I was reminded of
Böcklin. Hemmed in by the island's ancient cemetery walls, the tall
cypresses became indistinguishable from one another in the oozing
fog. They gently swayed in the lagoon breeze, like phantoms, the
spirits of the dead beneath them. Looming up from the ground,
it seemed the trees were shadows cast upright, as if the heaven's
bright rays beamed from below. We don't see things are they are, we
see things as we are. The soft fog enveloped us.

Everything feels lighter, less severe in Venice, you conclude your
problems aren't really real, or at least they aren't lasting. Its
enchantment captures you without your notice, and only when
you're fully submerged in your slumber do you realise you're
dreaming. And yet, your dream is where you stand and this city
is your trance. Marine melancholy streaming from the sublime
sadness of the sea ignites spiritual reveries. Yet the atmosphere isn't
mournful for the days of glory past, it is grateful, with awe and
idealism. Even the lampposts in St Mark's square are rose tinted.
Brodsky once proposed that beauty is a by-product of an often-
ordinary pursuit, but here, this extraordinary beauty is a product
of extraordinary pursuits. Your enduring magnificence helps me
indulge in my sheer insignificance.

In the 15C, the world population was a mere fraction of todays (in fact, one twentieth) and this contributes to my state of irrelevance. One out of eight billion feels disposable, replaceable, moot. And here – in Venice – a testament to the celebration of beauty by the comparable few, one feels incongruous as well. At the minimum, I am grateful that humanity has had the acumen to cradle and preserve this splendor, albeit in decaying grandeur. Venice, a barely buoyant galleon, overloaded with treasure but abandoned by its ancient masters, allows us to marvel at it in awe and envy.

By the second day you forget the noise of traffic. Lapping waters on the stairs descend directly into the lagoon, no obstructing parapet, no impediments. As if Venice calls out in mute, soft persuasions for you to shed your human skin, inviting your amphibian self to take to the water. As if, when my foot hits the first step, my fingers would web; as my foot hits the second, gills would reveal themselves on my neck; and as my flippered feet hit the water on the third, my skin would scale all over and I'll glide into the lagoon, cold-blooded and buoyant.

Everything is a feast for the eyes. Perhaps that's why people are walking slower, vexed by the need to look down at their phones for navigation - most of which is inaccurate or redundant. Many trails are unmapped, or lead to dead ends. The winding, narrow streets, parallel to life. All of a sudden you may become lost, and you can't quite remember how or when, for it all happened quite gradually. You were quite sure of your bearings, until suddenly, you're not. And here you're facing water, the infinite. You re-trace your steps until you see something more familiar, then, being careful not to repeat the same mistakes, you make a different turn, hoping for the best, hoping to reach your intended destination. Or perhaps, you've decided against the initial plan and begin your journey anew, with different intentions, as you're now quite sure the thing you wanted in the first place was just fool's gold. Above everything, because Venice remains the same, you're forced to reflect on the changes within you. And what a year it's been.

Venice